MW01296957

# " *Easy* "

# Watermelon
# Carvings

By Lonnie T. Lynch

*Learn how to create watermelon carvings that will be the hit of any party.*

# Publishing & Marketing

Press Books are available at quantity discounts when used to promote or sell product.
To place an order, or for information, please write to:

© Copyright 2012
Lonnie Lynch
All Rights Reserved
9415 Commonwealth Ave.
Jacksonville, FL 32220

*Or visit our Internet Web Site: www.lonnielynch.com*

Library of Congress Cataloging in process.
Published in the United States by
Lonnie T. Lynch

Distributor

© 2012 CreateSpace. All rights reserved.
ISBN-13: 978-1468199116

ISBN-10: 1468199110

# Acknowledgments

I would like to dedicate this book to my very special mother, Joyce Dee Agee, who raised five kids and never gave up.

**Special Recognition to**
Steve Galluzi Executive Chef Pete's Boca Raton
George Galluzi Former Chef U.S. Military Academy at West Point

I would like to thank George Galluzi for sharing his famous saying,

*"Don't be a jack of all trades be a specialist in one."*

Henrî Boubee-Executive Corporate Chef Ritz Carlton
Special thanks to the Boca Raton Resort and Beach Club; a 5-Star, World-Class Resort, where I created my first book and to my good friend always Chef Garde Manger Sergio Jean
Bob Barry, my good friend always, I could not have done these projects if not for your valuable help and guidance.

Good luck and thanks to all of you!

Cover Design Art
Shutterstock Green Photo 13798714 Shutterstock Images LLC

# Table of Contents

# The Art of Turning an Ordinary Watermelon Into an Elegant Carvings

## • Weddings • Holidays • Tropical Themes • Special Occasions •

For elegance and drama, borrow the tradition of serving a colorful and elegant carvings. A well designed, watermelon carving will contribute greatly to an air of elegance and soft romance, as well as being a great way to personalize your special day.

Food displays have traditionally been used over the years to decorate the dinner table. Both fresh and dried fruit and vegetables are very popular as decorative items, being relatively inexpensive and extremely colorful.

A food display serves not only as an attractive and decorative part of the presentation, but can also set the theme for certain types of dinner parties. Every good food presentation should have a central focal show point. At the same time, it must enhance the natural beauty of the foods prepared. By using food as the focal point, the display piece could also become part of the meal itself, which would then unify the whole presentation.

A watermelon can be transformed into a versatile and attractive centerpiece for any display you may want to create.

By using the simple, step-by-step guidelines presented in this book, anyone can take a watermelon and use it to enhance his or her presentation. In this book I will show you techniques that will enable you to carve whatever design you want on a watermelon. By using your imagination, you can then use other foods to create that special theme for any dinner party. The entire presentation will reflect not only your creative talents but will turn any dinner, buffet or picnic into a very special event. Presented here are only a few sample ideas, all of which I have done myself. Once you learn how I've created my displays, the rest is up to you.

### Be creative and have a good time!

# "Easy" Melon Carvings

**The Boca News/Essentials Carvings: From melons come palm trees, parrots and sailfish.**

Over 50 artistic culinary melon designs that everyone will love! Easy-to-follow hand illustrated instructions for honeydew and cantaloupe carvings. In this book, I will share with you easy methods and culinary know-how accumulated over the years, to help set the theme for many different types of holidays, special functions and parties for all to enjoy.

**Special Occasion Theme Carvings:** Classical Vase • Classical Swan • Neuvell Swan • Classical Wedding Bell • Kissing Doves with Wedding Bell • Exquisite Swan • "I Love You" • "I Love You" Swan Heads • "I Love You" Kissing Swans • Sweetheart Kissing Doves • Masterpiece Swan
**Holiday Theme Carvings:** Jewish Star of David • Holiday Christmas Reindeer • Holiday Christmas Tree • Holiday Christmas Bulb • America "USA" • Fourth of July Liberty Bell • St. Patrick's Shamrock and Pot O' Gold • Christmas Bulb Vase
**Tropical Theme Carvings:** Swordfish with Banner • Nautical Anchor and Wreath • Pink Flamingo and Palm Tree • Tropical Fish and Seaweed • Banners with Dolphin • Key West Claw, Fish Tail and Anchor • Nautical Palm Tree • Jumping Sailfish • Circus Seal with a Ball • Saint and Tropical Bird • Swordfish with Banner • Angelfish Fish with Seaweed • Three Jumping Dolphins • Scallop Shell and Palm Tree • Seahorse with Seaweed • Nautical Anchor Vase
**Oriental Theme Carving:** Good Luck Sign & Chinese Lantern • Oriental Rising Sun • Oriental Fan Vase • Oriental Lantern Vase • Oriental Sign Vase • Mythical Dragon Honeydew
**Other Theme Carvings:** Swan Vase Flower Holder • Graceful Dove on Flower • Southwestern Coyote and Moon • Southwestern Cactus • Smiling Quarter Moon with Star • Honeydew Vase with Cantaloupe Flower • Fantastic Cantaloupe Turtle • Ind Letters

List Price: $7.95 - 6" x 9" (15.24 x 22.86 cm) 116 pages
ISBN-13: 978-1468161120 (CreateSpace-Assigned)
ISBN-10: 1468161121
Cooking / Entertaining

# Watermelon Picking and Varieties

Many new varieties of watermelons have been developed in recent years. Yellow and seedless types are finding an increasing share of the specialty watermelon

Firm, symmetrical watermelons with dull rinds. Test for ripeness by tapping with your knuckle; you should hear a hollow sound. Look for a pale, yellowish area on the skin where the melon rested on the ground while ripening; if this is missing, the melon was picked prematurely and will not be as sweet. Well-grown, ripe melons should split open as soon as the knife cuts through the rind. The meat should be firm, a deep red, and free from white streaks.

### Charleston Gray Watermelon

This is a long fruit, weighing 28-35 pounds. Rind is light grayish-green with darker green veins. Flesh is bright red, crisp and sweet.

### Crimson Sweet Watermelon

Developed from the Charleston Gray, this is light green in color with dark stripes.

### Jubilee Watermelon

An oblong fruit, the Jubilee weighs an average of 30-35 pounds. Rind coloring is light green with dark green stripes and bright red, firm flesh.

### Klondike Watermelon

Striped light green with irregular dark green stripes, this variety is medium large, oblong in shape and weighs about 27 pounds. Flesh is scarlet.

### Sugar Baby Watermelon

A small watermelon weighing only eight to ten pounds on average. Sugar Baby's rind coloring is dark green with indistinct darker veining or medium green with darker veining. It has medium red, firm and crisp flesh.

### Grades of Watermelons

Grades for watermelon are: U.S. Fancy; U.S. No. 1 and U.S. No. 2. The grades conform to the U.S. Department of Agriculture's policy of establishing uniform grade names for fresh fruits and vegetables.as a partnership rank second along with Texas.

## Other Watermelon Types

Yellow Baby (hybrid-yellow flesh, 6 to 10 pounds)
Yellow Doll (hybrid-yellow flesh, 6 to 10 pounds)
Crimson Sweet (red, 20 to 25 pounds)
Madera (hybrid-red, 14 to 22 pounds)
Parker (hybrid-red, 22 to 25 pounds)
Sangria (hybrid-red, 22 to 26 pounds)
Sunny's Pride (hybrid-red, 20 to 22 pounds)
Sweet Favorite (hybrid-red, 20 pounds)

## Seedless Watermelons

Cotton Candy (red, 15 to 20 pounds)
Crimson Trio (red, 14 to 16 pounds)
Honey Heart (yellow flesh, 8 to 10 pounds)
Jack of Hearts (red, 14 to 18 pounds)
Nova (red, 15 to 17 pounds)
Queen of Hearts (red, 12 to 16 pounds)
Tiffany (red, 14 to 22 pounds).

## Care of Watermelons

At temperatures of 32° - 50° Fahrenheit, watermelons are subject to chill injury. After one week at 32° F., they will develop an off-flavor and become pitted. At 32° to 50° F., they lose color. At higher temperatures, they decay. Clean outside of watermelon with cool water before cutting as you would any fruit. Holding watermelon at room temperature can improve flavor and coloring.
The inside of a watermelon should display good, crisp red flesh. Melons should not be mealy or water soaked. Cover cut surface of watermelon loosely with plastic wrap to prevent flesh from becoming mushy.

## Watermelon Availability

March through October is the heaviest volume. Florida is the leader in the production of watermelon due to their southern location and size. California and Arizona as a partnership rank second along with Texas. Many other Southern states follow. Watermelons need plenty of heat, good soil and abundant water to flourish; the West has it all!
Watermelons can be produced almost year round in California and Arizona. The geographic diversity of both states allows the growing windows for watermelons to move throughout the region.

# Watermelon Carving, Stencil Usage Instructions

This section is designed to outline the ideas and techniques, that will make using your melon stencils simple and safe.

Leaving the watermelon out side of refrigerator for at least 6 hours will help remove moisture and will make the tape.

Pick a theme and print out a copy of the stencil you want to use!

Trim the copy to a workable size. By cutting slits into the edge of the design, it will be easier to attach to the melon's curved surface.

### Stencil Usage Instructions Figure 1.

Start by wiping excess moisture off of the melon portion you select for carving (make sure your design is scaled to the right size for the portion you have chosen). Fasten stencil securely to melon using Scotch tape. Using an X-Acto knife, as shown above, cut a design into the melon using your stencil as a guide, making sure not to cut too deeply at this point. Attach more Scotch tape as needed to keep stencil secure until design is complete. Remove stencil and continue carving, using detailed instructions in stencil section.

### X-Acto Knife Detailed Instructions Figure 2.

This is the tool you use to make fine detailed cuts into the melon using your stencil. Other useful tools are shown on pages 12-13-14-15.

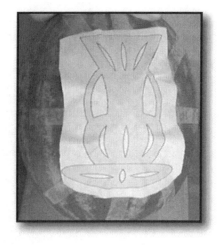

# How to Use a Grid to Reduce or Enlarge a Stencil

If you need to enlarge or reduce the designs, the procedure is relatively easy. Using a ruler, draw a square box around the design and divide into even boxes.

Next, using a ruler, draw a square box the size of the design that you would like to enlarge or reduce. Next, measure the sides and divide into the number of squares in the design that you would like to reduce or enlarge.

Mark box and draw lines to correspond with exact amount of squares, (example is 15 across and 13 up and down) in the smaller or larger design. Each block should be regarded separately, and the lines of the design that fall in corresponding blocks should be duplicated, (traced) in the stencils new grid. When finished, you will have an accurately enlarged or reduced pattern design.

### Grid Enlargement Hints

Grid enlargement is very simple, yet complicated. But, by using the grid system you can take a small drawing and enlarge or reduce as needed.

### Enlarged Stencil Instructions Figure 1.

Accurately enlarged or reduced pattern design. Example grids are 15 across and 13 up and down squares. Horse's Head Carving, page 59.

### Reduced Stencil Instructions Figure 2.

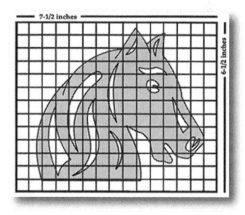

# Watermelon Sculpting Tool Information Section

Here are some points given below on fruit carving tools and their special usage. Your efforts will be rewarded when your guests and friends don't stop talking about your creation!

### Paring Knife Tool

A paring knife is a small knife with a plain edge blade that is ideal for peeling and other small or intricate work. The handle is perfectly proportioned with a open flow to accommodate the hand while improving convenience and safety for the user.

### V-Tool Decorator Tool

This tool is used to make large and small "V's". (Size of "V's" depends on the depth that the tool is used.)
I got my v-shaped tool at a local flea market, but you might be able to find one at a kitchen or housewares store. Though it might take a little longer, a small sharp knife would work as well.

### X-Acto Knife Tool

The X-ACTO precision knife is the original cutting tool for any application requiring a precise, accurate cut. The X-Acto knife may be called a utility knife, but it is actually a short, sharp blade mounted on a pen-like aluminum body, used for crafting and hobbies.

### Channel Knife Tool

A commonly used bar tool, the channel knife is a small peeler with a metal tooth on one end used for making long, thin garnishes such as citrus twists. This tool is used for cutting designs in fruit as it removes the outside flesh.

### Melon Baller Tool

Used to make melon balls, as well as designs on fruit. Available in plain, fluted and oval styles from 1/8" to 1".

**Easy carving instructions!**

# Watermelon Carving Step-by-Step Instructions

### Creating Culinary Carvings Figure 1.

Start by making a copy of the pattern (Stencil) you want to use. Wipe watermelon dry. Examine your watermelon to determine the best place to carve design.

Secure stencil against watermelon by using Scotch tape, that does not slide, see page 10 for more details on stencil usage Classical Vase Carving, page 105.

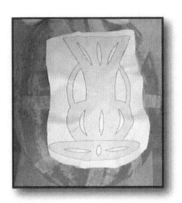

### Creating Culinary Carvings Figure 2.

Using X-Acto knife or paring knife, make cuts along pattern (stencil) lines, working from the inside of pattern to the outside of the pattern when cutting.

Using more Scotch tape as you carve will makes things easier.

# Watermelon Carving Step-by-Step Instructions, Continued

### Creating Culinary Carvings Figure 3.

Remove pattern, (Stencil) tape and start cutting away the edges of the background on the outside of the pattern that you just traced on watermelon, making sure not to go too deep, or too far outside pattern just now. Carve a little at a time from the edges to even it out. Safety Tip Wear a glove to protect your hand(s).

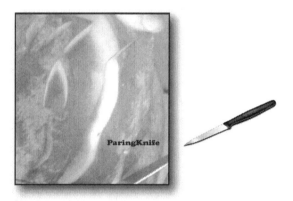

### Creating Culinary Carvings Figure 4.

Start carving out inside of fine lines, cleaning up area as you go along.
Holding knife at an angle makes cutting easier.
Only 30 minutes to this beautiful and delicious centerpiece!

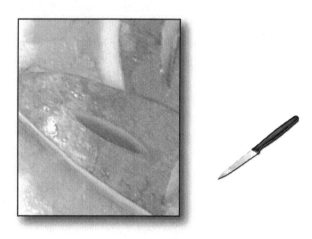

# Watermelon Carving Step-by-Step Instructions, Continues

### Creating Culinary Carvings Figure 5.

Now, prepare for carving edges of background. Make sure not to go too far around watermelon. Show only a little bit of red flesh, the V-Tool cuts will show more later. Smooth out and clean up shape of pattern.

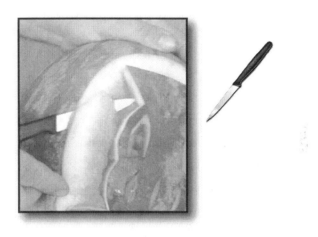

### Creating Culinary Carvings Figure 6.

With the special v-shaped knife, cut grooves in background all the way around the pattern, this will create a unique looking (scalloped effect) picture frame around the pattern. Be careful not to cut into carving and pull it loose. If you don't have a V-Tool a sharp knife will work just fine.

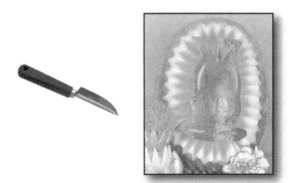

# Watermelon Carving Step-by-Step Instructions, Continued

### Creating Culinary Carvings Figure 7.

Using a paring knife clean up entire watermelon carving. Straighten and smooth all of the edges and make sure you can see red flesh inside all inner cuts.

Next cut just enough of the bottom from the watermelon to to make it stand up and keep from rocking.

### Creating Culinary Carvings Figure 8.

### Elegant Colors of a Watermelon

Pay attention to colors. By shaving just below the outside green flesh of the watermelon you can obtain a white color.

Practice using different colors for contrast.

### Color Code Depth Chart

A = Outside Green Flesh Color
B = Inside Red Flesh Color
C = Inside White Flesh Color

# Watermelon Carving Decorating Instructions

A midnight buffet on a cruise draws people with cameras for a look at the elaborate garnishes and carvings. So now you to will have people taking pictures of your parties buffet table. After you have finished carving the watermelon centerpiece, you may add decoration to complete the presentation.

Serving a great looking carving will give you a feeling of satisfaction! Choose textures, colors,and shapes that complement each other.

### We eat with our eyes . . . Then our palate .

Food beautifully presented with dazzling colors and shapes can really enhance any party. Even you can practice the art of a spectacular food presentation with a few simple tricks.

Start by cutting off a small portion of the watermelon to act as a base. You now have to make the sculptors look good. It's by no way complete, just a starter. Using background and support material such as cantaloupe crowns and ferns, as well as other items listed on page 19, you can decorate the serving plate or mirror. By carefully looking at the carving itself, you can easily see what can be done to improve the appearance.

## Dazzling Colors of Food

The color of food is an integral part of our culture and enjoyment of life. Who would deny the mouth-watering appeal of a deep-pink strawberry on a hot summer day. For extra-special effects, garnish the carving with edible flowers and/or berries fastened with toothpicks.

## Decorating Culinary Carvings Figure 9.

This final touch will create a very appealing presentation for all to enjoy. For the best impression, some dishes look much brighter in their natural way, that is why it is not neccasary to overload them with excessive decorating.

### Clean, simple, elegant and beautiful.

# Watermelon Carving Repairs and Alterations

**As you, as an artist, start to practice Carving Watermelon Carvings you will undoubtedly run into various challenges.
Be patient help is at hand!**

This section on repairs and modifications will give you ideas and techniques on repairing flaws that are bound to occur in the course of each project.

Patience and practice are the two indispensable virtues in learning, and mastering, this craft.

### Alterations Hints and Tips

• Wooden toothpicks and skewers can be used to re-align pieces of watermelon carvings that fall off.

• Flowers, ferns and (fresh) fruit can be used to cover up minor flaws if need be.

• By using imagination and careful, gentle work habits, you can repair just about anything, no matter how major!

**Good luck and BE CAREFUL! Patience and Practice!**

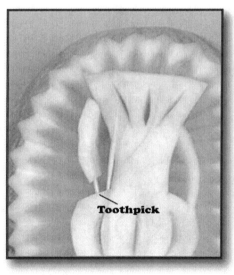

Toothpick

# Watermelon Carving Hints & Tips

Before you begin to create your garnishes, you will need some simple tools. A good paring knife and a small, sharp, serrated knife can be very helpful. As always, make sure your knives are sharp and in good condition; most people cut themselves with dull knives, not sharp ones.

## Patience and Practice

Always use the proper equipment. Try to use the correct tool for the task at hand! A dull knife is more dangerous than a sharp one! Knives and tools should be kept sharp at all times.
Always hold the knives firmly, and always remember that patience and practice will take you a long, long way.

## Exotic Fruits Decorations

Exotic fruits will make a perfect decorations. Pineapples, bananas, melons, kiwis and watermelons will decorate your table in the most beautiful way.

## Support and Background Materials

Here's a starter list of some basic Support and Background Materials To create a beautiful composition, you need big, even and solid garnishes.

**Fresh Ferns**
**Flowers (both fresh and dried)**
**Pineapples and the Tops**
**Mint Leaves**
**Leaf Lettuce**
**Radicchio Leaves**
**Oranges (cut into crowns)**
**Toothpicks (wooden)**
**Toothpick Frills (wooden)**
**Cantaloupe (cut into crowns)**
**Honeydew Melon (cut into crowns)**
**Whole Cloves (used as eyes)**
**Fresh Strawberries**
**Lemon and Lime Crowns**
**Maraschino Cherries**
**Etc. Etc.**

• Weddings • Holidays • Tropical Themes •
• Special Occasions •

# Stencil Design Section

# Anchor and Wreath Carving

Large oblong watermelon needed such as a Charleston Gray. When selecting which side of the watermelon to carve, make sure to use the green and clean side.

Print the stencil on the next page and trim the stencil to a workable size. By cutting slits into the edge of the design, it will be easier to attach to the melon's curved surface.

*See "Watermelon Carving Stencil Usage Instructions" for using stencils, on page 10.*
*Start by using the "Watermelon Carving Step-by-Step Instructions" on pages 13-16.*

## Using Color Code Depth Chart (Colors of a Watermelon )

By using the color code depth chart shown below on the watermelon, you will know how deep to carve, and which colors to make certain cuts.

*Pay attention to colors. Practice using different colors for contrast.*

## Color Code Depth Chart

A = Outside Green Flesh Color
B = Inside Red Flesh Color
C = Inside White Flesh Color
(White color can be made by carving just below the green color outside flesh.)

## Decorating Your Watermelon Carving

Start by using the "Watermelon Carving Decorating Instructions" and ideas on page 17, and by using what you have on hand.

## Special Carving Instructions

Carve Anchor and Crown in color code "A".
Carve Wreath in color code "C".
Carve all inside lines in color code "B".

# Tropical Angelfish Carving

Large oblong watermelon needed such as a Charleston Gray. When selecting which side of the watermelon to carve, make sure to use the green and clean side.
Print the stencil on the next page and trim the stencil to a workable size. By cutting slits into the edge of the design, it will be easier to attach to the melon's curved surface.

*See "Watermelon Carving Stencil Usage Instructions" for using stencils, on page 10.*
*Start by using the "Watermelon Carving Step-by-Step Instructions" on pages 13-16.*

## Using Color Code Depth Chart (Colors of a Watermelon )

By using the color code depth chart shown below on the watermelon, you will know how deep to carve, and which colors to make certain cuts.

***Pay attention to colors. Practice using different colors for contrast.***

## Color Code Depth Chart

> A = Outside Green Flesh Color
> B = Inside Red Flesh Color
> C = Inside White Flesh Color
> > (White color can be made by carving just below the green color outside flesh.)

## Decorating Your Watermelon Carving

Start by using the "Watermelon Carving Decorating Instructions" and ideas on page 17, and by using what you have on hand.

## Special Carving Instructions

> Carve Angel Fish in color code "C".
> Carve all inside lines in color code "B".

# Chinese Lantern & Good Luck Sign Carving

Large oblong watermelon needed such as a Charleston Gray. When selecting which side of the watermelon to carve, make sure to use the green and clean side.

Print the stencil on the next page and trim the stencil to a workable size. By cutting slits into the edge of the design, it will be easier to attach to the melon's curved surface.

*See "Watermelon Carving Stencil Usage Instructions" for using stencils, on page 10.*
*Start by using the "Watermelon Carving Step-by-Step Instructions" on pages 13-16.*

## Using Color Code Depth Chart (Colors of a Watermelon )

By using the color code depth chart shown below on the watermelon, you will know how deep to carve, and which colors to make certain cuts.

*Pay attention to colors. Practice using different colors for contrast.*

## Color Code Depth Chart

> A = Outside Green Flesh Color
> B = Inside Red Flesh Color
> C = Inside White Flesh Color
> (White color can be made by carving just below the green color outside flesh.)

## Decorating Your Watermelon Carving

Start by using the "Watermelon Carving Decorating Instructions" and ideas on page 17, and by using what you have on hand.

## Special Carving Instructions

> Carve Good Luck Sign in color code "A".
> Carve Lantern in color code "C".
> Carve all inside lines in color code "B".

# Chinese Writing "Hello" Carving

Large oblong watermelon needed such as a Charleston Gray. When selecting which side of the watermelon to carve, make sure to use the green and clean side.

Print the stencil on the next page and trim the stencil to a workable size. By cutting slits into the edge of the design, it will be easier to attach to the melon's curved surface.

*See "Watermelon Carving Stencil Usage Instructions" for using stencils, on page 10.*
*Start by using the "Watermelon Carving Step-by-Step Instructions" on pages 13-16.*

## Using Color Code Depth Chart (Colors of a Watermelon )

By using the color code depth chart shown below on the watermelon, you will know how deep to carve, and which colors to make certain cuts.

*Pay attention to colors. Practice using different colors for contrast.*

## Color Code Depth Chart

A = Outside Green Flesh Color
B = Inside Red Flesh Color
C = Inside White Flesh Color
(White color can be made by carving just below the green color outside flesh.)

## Decorating Your Watermelon Carving

Start by using the "Watermelon Carving Decorating Instructions" and ideas on page 17, and by using what you have on hand.

## Special Carving Instructions

Carve Chinese Writing "Hello" in color code "A" or "C".

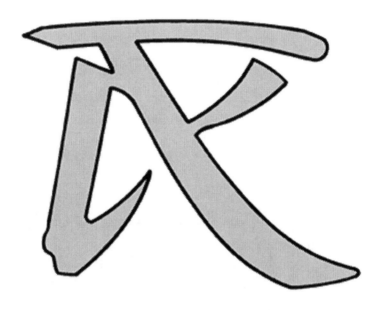

# Christmas Bulb Carving

Large oblong watermelon needed such as a Charleston Gray. When select-ing which side of the watermelon to carve, make sure to use the green and clean side.

Print the stencil on the next page and trim the stencil to a workable size. By cutting slits into the edge of the design, it will be easier to attach to the melon's curved surface.

*See "Watermelon Carving Stencil Usage Instructions" for using stencils, on page 10.*
*Start by using the "Watermelon Carving Step-by-Step Instructions" on pages 13-16.*

## Using Color Code Depth Chart (Colors of a Watermelon )

By using the color code depth chart shown below on the watermelon, you will know how deep to carve, and which colors to make certain cuts.

***Pay attention to colors. Practice using different colors for contrast.***

## Color Code Depth Chart

A = Outside Green Flesh Color
B = Inside Red Flesh Color
C = Inside White Flesh Color
    (White color can be made by carving just below the green color outside flesh.)

## Decorating Your Watermelon Carving

Start by using the "Watermelon Carving Decorating Instructions" and ideas on page 17, and by using what you have on hand.

## Special Carving Instructions

Carve Christmas Bulb in color code "C".
Carve all inside lines in color code "B".

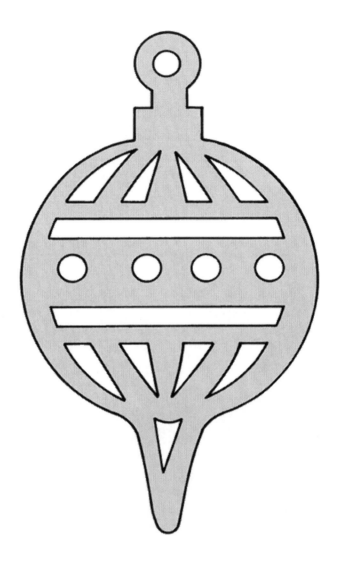

# Christmas Candy Cane w/Bulb & Star Carving

Large oblong watermelon needed such as a Charleston Gray. When selecting which side of the watermelon to carve, make sure to use the green and clean side.

Print the stencil on the next page and trim the stencil to a workable size. By cutting slits into the edge of the design, it will be easier to attach to the melon's curved surface.

*See "Watermelon Carving Stencil Usage Instructions" for using stencils, on page 10.*
*Start by using the "Watermelon Carving Step-by-Step Instructions" on pages 13-16.*

## Using Color Code Depth Chart (Colors of a Watermelon )

By using the color code depth chart shown below on the watermelon, you will know how deep to carve, and which colors to make certain cuts.

***Pay attention to colors. Practice using different colors for contrast.***

## Color Code Depth Chart

A = Outside Green Flesh Color
B = Inside Red Flesh Color
C = Inside White Flesh Color
(White color can be made by carving just below the green color outside flesh.)

## Decorating Your Watermelon Carving

Start by using the "Watermelon Carving Decorating Instructions" and ideas on page 17, and by using what you have on hand.

## Special Carving Instructions

Carve Christmas Candy Cane w/Bulb & Star in color code "A".
Carve Bulb & Star in color code "C".
Carve all inside lines in color code "B".

# Christmas Tree Carving

Large oblong watermelon needed such as a Charleston Gray. When selecting which side of the watermelon to carve, make sure to use the green and clean side.
Print the stencil on the next page and trim the stencil to a workable size. By cutting slits into the edge of the design, it will be easier to attach to the melon's curved surface.

*See "Watermelon Carving Stencil Usage Instructions" for using stencils, on page 10.*
*Start by using the "Watermelon Carving Step-by-Step Instructions" on pages 13-16.*

## Using Color Code Depth Chart (Colors of a Watermelon )

By using the color code depth chart shown below on the watermelon, you will know how deep to carve, and which colors to make certain cuts.

*Pay attention to colors. Practice using different colors for contrast.*

## Color Code Depth Chart

A = Outside Green Flesh Color
B = Inside Red Flesh Color
C = Inside White Flesh Color
(White color can be made by carving just below the green color outside flesh.)

## Decorating Your Watermelon Carving

Start by using the "Watermelon Carving Decorating Instructions" and ideas on page 17, and by using what you have on hand.

## Special Carving Instructions

Carve Christmas Tree in color code "A" or "C".
Carve all inside lines in color code "B".

# Circus Seal and Dolphin Carving

Large oblong watermelon needed such as a Charleston Gray. When selecting which side of the watermelon to carve, make sure to use the green and clean side.

Print the stencil on the next page and trim the stencil to a workable size. By cutting slits into the edge of the design, it will be easier to attach to the melon's curved surface.

*See "Watermelon Carving Stencil Usage Instructions" for using stencils, on page 10.*
*Start by using the "Watermelon Carving Step-by-Step Instructions" on pages 13-16.*

## Using Color Code Depth Chart (Colors of a Watermelon )

By using the color code depth chart shown below on the watermelon, you will know how deep to carve, and which colors to make certain cuts.

***Pay attention to colors. Practice using different colors for contrast.***

## Color Code Depth Chart

    A = Outside Green Flesh Color
    B = Inside Red Flesh Color
    C = Inside White Flesh Color
        (White color can be made by carving just below the green
        color outside flesh.)

## Decorating Your Watermelon Carving

Start by using the "Watermelon Carving Decorating Instructions" and ideas on page 17, and by using what you have on hand.

## Special Carving Instructions

    Carve Dolphin Circus Seal in color code "C".
    Carve Base and Balls in color code "A".
    Carve all inside lines in color code "B".

# Kissing Swans on a Heart Carving

Large oblong watermelon needed such as a Charleston Gray. When selecting which side of the watermelon to carve, make sure to use the green and clean side.

Print the stencil on the next page and trim the stencil to a workable size. By cutting slits into the edge of the design, it will be easier to attach to the melon's curved surface.

*See "Watermelon Carving Stencil Usage Instructions" for using stencils, on page 10.*
*Start by using the "Watermelon Carving Step-by-Step Instructions" on pages 13-16.*

## Using Color Code Depth Chart (Colors of a Watermelon )

By using the color code depth chart shown below on the watermelon, you will know how deep to carve, and which colors to make certain cuts.

*Pay attention to colors. Practice using different colors for contrast.*

## Color Code Depth Chart

A = Outside Green Flesh Color
B = Inside Red Flesh Color
C = Inside White Flesh Color
(White color can be made by carving just below the green color outside flesh.)

## Decorating Your Watermelon Carving

Start by using the "Watermelon Carving Decorating Instructions" and ideas on page 17, and by using what you have on hand.

## Special Carving Instructions

Carve Kissing Swans on a Heart in color code "C".
Carve Heart in color code "C".
Carve all inside lines in color code "B".

# Dolphin on Waves Carving

Large oblong watermelon needed such as a Charleston Gray. When selecting which side of the watermelon to carve, make sure to use the green and clean side.

Print the stencil on the next page and trim the stencil to a workable size. By cutting slits into the edge of the design, it will be easier to attach to the melon's curved surface.

*See "Watermelon Carving Stencil Usage Instructions" for using stencils, on page 10.*
*Start by using the "Watermelon Carving Step-by-Step Instructions" on pages 13-16.*

## Using Color Code Depth Chart (Colors of a Watermelon )

By using the color code depth chart shown below on the watermelon, you will know how deep to carve, and which colors to make certain cuts.

***Pay attention to colors. Practice using different colors for contrast.***

## Color Code Depth Chart

A = Outside Green Flesh Color
B = Inside Red Flesh Color
C = Inside White Flesh Color
(White color can be made by carving just below the green color outside flesh.)

## Decorating Your Watermelon Carving

Start by using the "Watermelon Carving Decorating Instructions" and ideas on page 17, and by using what you have on hand.

## Special Carving Instructions

Carve Dolphin in color code "C".
Carve Waves in color code "A".
Carve all inside lines in color code "B".

# Double Palm Trees Carving

Large oblong watermelon needed such as a Charleston Gray. When selecting which side of the watermelon to carve, make sure to use the green and clean side.

Print the stencil on the next page and trim the stencil to a workable size. By cutting slits into the edge of the design, it will be easier to attach to the melon's curved surface.

*See "Watermelon Carving Stencil Usage Instructions" for using stencils, on page 10.*
*Start by using the "Watermelon Carving Step-by-Step Instructions" on pages 13-16.*

## Using Color Code Depth Chart (Colors of a Watermelon )

By using the color code depth chart shown below on the watermelon, you will know how deep to carve, and which colors to make certain cuts.

*Pay attention to colors. Practice using different colors for contrast.*

## Color Code Depth Chart

A = Outside Green Flesh Color
B = Inside Red Flesh Color
C = Inside White Flesh Color
(White color can be made by carving just below the green color outside flesh.)

## Decorating Your Watermelon Carving

Start by using the "Watermelon Carving Decorating Instructions" and ideas on page 17, and by using what you have on hand.

## Special Carving Instructions

Carve Double Palm Trees in color code "A" or "C".
Carve all inside lines in color code "B".

# Flying Dove Carving

Large oblong watermelon needed such as a Charleston Gray. When select-ing which side of the watermelon to carve, make sure to use the green and clean side.

Print the stencil on the next page and trim the stencil to a workable size. By cutting slits into the edge of the design, it will be easier to attach to the melon's curved surface.

*See "Watermelon Carving Stencil Usage Instructions" for using stencils, on page 10.*
*Start by using the "Watermelon Carving Step-by-Step Instructions" on pages 13-16.*

## Using Color Code Depth Chart (Colors of a Watermelon )

By using the color code depth chart shown below on the watermelon, you will know how deep to carve, and which colors to make certain cuts.

*Pay attention to colors. Practice using different colors for contrast.*

## Color Code Depth Chart

    A = Outside Green Flesh Color
    B = Inside Red Flesh Color
    C = Inside White Flesh Color
        (White color can be made by carving just below the green
        color outside flesh.)

## Decorating Your Watermelon Carving

Start by using the "Watermelon Carving Decorating Instructions" and ideas on page 17, and by using what you have on hand.

## Special Carving Instructions

    Carve Flying Dove in color code "A" or "C".
    Carve all inside lines in color code "B".

# Mythical Dragon Head Carving

Large oblong watermelon needed such as a Charleston Gray. When selecting which side of the watermelon to carve, make sure to use the green and clean side.

Print the stencil on the next page and trim the stencil to a workable size. By cutting slits into the edge of the design, it will be easier to attach to the melon's curved surface.

*See "Watermelon Carving Stencil Usage Instructions" for using stencils, on page 10.*
*Start by using the "Watermelon Carving Step-by-Step Instructions" on pages 13-16.*

## Using Color Code Depth Chart (Colors of a Watermelon )

By using the color code depth chart shown below on the watermelon, you will know how deep to carve, and which colors to make certain cuts.

*Pay attention to colors. Practice using different colors for contrast.*

## Color Code Depth Chart

> A = Outside Green Flesh Color
> B = Inside Red Flesh Color
> C = Inside White Flesh Color
>   (White color can be made by carving just below the green color outside flesh.)

## Decorating Your Watermelon Carving

Start by using the "Watermelon Carving Decorating Instructions" and ideas on page 17, and by using what you have on hand.

## Special Carving Instructions

Carve Mythical Dragon Head in color code "A" or "C".
Carve all inside lines in color code "B".

# American Eagle Carving

Large oblong watermelon needed such as a Charleston Gray. When selecting which side of the watermelon to carve, make sure to use the green and clean side.

Print the stencil on the next page and trim the stencil to a workable size. By cutting slits into the edge of the design, it will be easier to attach to the melon's curved surface.

*See "Watermelon Carving Stencil Usage Instructions" for using stencils, on page 10.*
*Start by using the "Watermelon Carving Step-by-Step Instructions" on pages 13-16.*

## Using Color Code Depth Chart (Colors of a Watermelon )

By using the color code depth chart shown below on the watermelon, you will know how deep to carve, and which colors to make certain cuts.

***Pay attention to colors. Practice using different colors for contrast.***

## Color Code Depth Chart

   A = Outside Green Flesh Color
   B = Inside Red Flesh Color
   C = Inside White Flesh Color
       (White color can be made by carving just below the green color outside flesh.)

## Decorating Your Watermelon Carving

Start by using the "Watermelon Carving Decorating Instructions" and ideas on page 17, and by using what you have on hand.

## Special Carving Instructions

   Carve Bald Eagle in color code "A" or "C".
   Carve all inside lines in color code "B".

# Easter Bunny Painting Egg Carving

Large oblong watermelon needed such as a Charleston Gray. When selecting which side of the watermelon to carve, make sure to use the green and clean side.

Print the stencil on the next page and trim the stencil to a workable size. By cutting slits into the edge of the design, it will be easier to attach to the melon's curved surface.

*See "Watermelon Carving Stencil Usage Instructions" for using stencils, on page 10.*
*Start by using the "Watermelon Carving Step-by-Step Instructions" on pages 13-16.*

## Using Color Code Depth Chart (Colors of a Watermelon )

By using the color code depth chart shown below on the watermelon, you will know how deep to carve, and which colors to make certain cuts.

***Pay attention to colors. Practice using different colors for contrast.***

## Color Code Depth Chart

A = Outside Green Flesh Color
B = Inside Red Flesh Color
C = Inside White Flesh Color
(White color can be made by carving just below the green color outside flesh.)

## Decorating Your Watermelon Carving

Start by using the "Watermelon Carving Decorating Instructions" and ideas on page 17, and by using what you have on hand.

## Special Carving Instructions

Carve Easter Bunny Painting in color code "C".
Carve Easter Egg in color code "A".
Carve all inside lines in color code "B".

# 4th of July Carving

Large oblong watermelon needed such as a Charleston Gray. When selecting which side of the watermelon to carve, make sure to use the green and clean side.

Print the stencil on the next page and trim the stencil to a workable size. By cutting slits into the edge of the design, it will be easier to attach to the melon's curved surface.

*See "Watermelon Carving Stencil Usage Instructions" for using stencils, on page 10.*
*Start by using the "Watermelon Carving Step-by-Step Instructions" on pages 13-16.*

## Using Color Code Depth Chart (Colors of a Watermelon )

By using the color code depth chart shown below on the watermelon, you will know how deep to carve, and which colors to make certain cuts.

*Pay attention to colors. Practice using different colors for contrast.*

## Color Code Depth Chart

A = Outside Green Flesh Color
B = Inside Red Flesh Color
C = Inside White Flesh Color
(White color can be made by carving just below the green color outside flesh.)

## Decorating Your Watermelon Carving

Start by using the "Watermelon Carving Decorating Instructions" and ideas on page 17, and by using what you have on hand.

## Special Carving Instructions

Carve "th and July" in color code "A".
Carve 4 and Star in color code "C".
Carve all inside lines in color code "B".

# Two Kissing Doves with Heart

Large oblong watermelon needed such as a Charleston Gray. When selecting which side of the watermelon to carve, make sure to use the green and clean side.

Print the stencil on the next page and trim the stencil to a workable size. By cutting slits into the edge of the design, it will be easier to attach to the melon's curved surface.

*See "Watermelon Carving Stencil Usage Instructions" for using stencils, on page 10.*
*Start by using the "Watermelon Carving Step-by-Step Instructions" on pages 13-16.*

## Using Color Code Depth Chart (Colors of a Watermelon )

By using the color code depth chart shown below on the watermelon, you will know how deep to carve, and which colors to make certain cuts.

*Pay attention to colors. Practice using different colors for contrast.*

## Color Code Depth Chart

A = Outside Green Flesh Color
B = Inside Red Flesh Color
C = Inside White Flesh Color
(White color can be made by carving just below the green color outside flesh.)

## Decorating Your Watermelon Carving

Start by using the "Watermelon Carving Decorating Instructions" and ideas on page 17, and by using what you have on hand.

## Special Carving Instructions

Carve Doves and Banner in color code "C".
Carve Heart in color code "A".
Carve all inside lines in color code "B".

# Horse's Head Carving

Large oblong watermelon needed such as a Charleston Gray. When selecting which side of the watermelon to carve, make sure to use the green and clean side.

Print the stencil on the next page and trim the stencil to a workable size. By cutting slits into the edge of the design, it will be easier to attach to the melon's curved surface.

*See "Watermelon Carving Stencil Usage Instructions" for using stencils, on page 10.*
*Start by using the "Watermelon Carving Step-by-Step Instructions" on pages 13-16.*

## Using Color Code Depth Chart (Colors of a Watermelon )

By using the color code depth chart shown below on the watermelon, you will know how deep to carve, and which colors to make certain cuts.

*Pay attention to colors. Practice using different colors for contrast.*

## Color Code Depth Chart

A = Outside Green Flesh Color
B = Inside Red Flesh Color
C = Inside White Flesh Color
(White color can be made by carving just below the green color outside flesh.)

## Decorating Your Watermelon Carving

Start by using the "Watermelon Carving Decorating Instructions" and ideas on page 17, and by using what you have on hand.

## Special Carving Instructions

Carve Horse's Head in color code "A" or "C".
Carve all inside lines in color code "B".

# Maine Lobster Carving

Large oblong watermelon needed such as a Charleston Gray. When selecting which side of the watermelon to carve, make sure to use the green and clean side.

Print the stencil on the next page and trim the stencil to a workable size. By cutting slits into the edge of the design, it will be easier to attach to the melon's curved surface.

*See "Watermelon Carving Stencil Usage Instructions" for using stencils, on page 10.*
*Start by using the "Watermelon Carving Step-by-Step Instructions" on pages 13-16.*

## Using Color Code Depth Chart (Colors of a Watermelon )

By using the color code depth chart shown below on the watermelon, you will know how deep to carve, and which colors to make certain cuts.

*Pay attention to colors. Practice using different colors for contrast.*

## Color Code Depth Chart

A = Outside Green Flesh Color
B = Inside Red Flesh Color
C = Inside White Flesh Color
(White color can be made by carving just below the green color outside flesh.)

## Decorating Your Watermelon Carving

Start by using the "Watermelon Carving Decorating Instructions" and ideas on page 17, and by using what you have on hand.

## Special Carving Instructions

Carve Maine Lobster in color code "A".
Carve all inside lines in color code "B".
Carve Maine Lobster in color code "C".

# Marlin with Sunset Carving

Large oblong watermelon needed such as a Charleston Gray. When selecting which side of the watermelon to carve, make sure to use the green and clean side.

Print the stencil on the next page and trim the stencil to a workable size. By cutting slits into the edge of the design, it will be easier to attach to the melon's curved surface.

*See "Watermelon Carving Stencil Usage Instructions" for using stencils, on page 10.*
*Start by using the "Watermelon Carving Step-by-Step Instructions" on pages 13-16.*

## Using Color Code Depth Chart (Colors of a Watermelon )

By using the color code depth chart shown below on the watermelon, you will know how deep to carve, and which colors to make certain cuts.

*Pay attention to colors. Practice using different colors for contrast.*

## Color Code Depth Chart

> A = Outside Green Flesh Color
> B = Inside Red Flesh Color
> C = Inside White Flesh Color
> > (White color can be made by carving just below the green color outside flesh.)

## Decorating Your Watermelon Carving

Start by using the "Watermelon Carving Decorating Instructions" and ideas on page 17, and by using what you have on hand.

## Special Carving Instructions

> Carve Marlin in color code "C".
> Carve Sunset in color code "A".
> Carve all inside lines in color code "B".

# Special Mom #1 Carving

Large oblong watermelon needed such as a Charleston Gray. When selecting which side of the watermelon to carve, make sure to use the green and clean side.

Print the stencil on the next page and trim the stencil to a workable size. By cutting slits into the edge of the design, it will be easier to attach to the melon's curved surface.

*See "Watermelon Carving Stencil Usage Instructions" for using stencils, on page 10.*

*Start by using the "Watermelon Carving Step-by-Step Instructions" on pages 13-16.*

## Using Color Code Depth Chart (Colors of a Watermelon )

By using the color code depth chart shown below on the watermelon, you will know how deep to carve, and which colors to make certain cuts.

*Pay attention to colors. Practice using different colors for contrast.*

## Color Code Depth Chart

A = Outside Green Flesh Color
B = Inside Red Flesh Color
C = Inside White Flesh Color
(White color can be made by carving just below the green color outside flesh.)

## Decorating Your Watermelon Carving

Start by using the "Watermelon Carving Decorating Instructions" and ideas on page 17, and by using what you have on hand.

## Special Carving Instructions

Carve Mom #1 Carving in color code "A" or "C".
Carve all inside lines in color code "B".

# Grand Nautical Carving

Large oblong watermelon needed such as a Charleston Gray. When selecting which side of the watermelon to carve, make sure to use the green and clean side.

Print the stencil on the next page and trim the stencil to a workable size. By cutting slits into the edge of the design, it will be easier to attach to the melon's curved surface.

*See "Watermelon Carving Stencil Usage Instructions" for using stencils, on page 10.*
*Start by using the "Watermelon Carving Step-by-Step Instructions" on pages 13-16.*

## Using Color Code Depth Chart (Colors of a Watermelon )

By using the color code depth chart shown below on the watermelon, you will know how deep to carve, and which colors to make certain cuts.

***Pay attention to colors. Practice using different colors for contrast.***

## Color Code Depth Chart

A = Outside Green Flesh Color
B = Inside Red Flesh Color
C = Inside White Flesh Color
   (White color can be made by carving just below the green color outside flesh.)

## Decorating Your Watermelon Carving

Start by using the "Watermelon Carving Decorating Instructions" and ideas on page 17, and by using what you have on hand.

## Special Carving Instructions

Carve Nautical Carving in color code "A" or "C".
Carve all inside lines and Anchor in color code "B".

# Tropical Parrot on Branch Carving

Large oblong watermelon needed such as a Charleston Gray. When selecting which side of the watermelon to carve, make sure to use the green and clean side.

Print the stencil on the next page and trim the stencil to a workable size. By cutting slits into the edge of the design, it will be easier to attach to the melon's curved surface.

*See "Watermelon Carving Stencil Usage Instructions" for using stencils, on page 10.*
*Start by using the "Watermelon Carving Step-by-Step Instructions" on pages 13-16.*

## Using Color Code Depth Chart (Colors of a Watermelon )

By using the color code depth chart shown below on the watermelon, you will know how deep to carve, and which colors to make certain cuts.

***Pay attention to colors. Practice using different colors for contrast.***

## Color Code Depth Chart

    A = Outside Green Flesh Color
    B = Inside Red Flesh Color
    C = Inside White Flesh Color
        (White color can be made by carving just below the green color outside flesh.)

## Decorating Your Watermelon Carving

Start by using the "Watermelon Carving Decorating Instructions" and ideas on page 17, and by using what you have on hand.

## Special Carving Instructions

    Carve Parrot on Branch in color code "A".
    Carve top left side of eye 1/6" below the color in color code "A".
    Carve all inside lines in color code "B".

# Pelican with Fish Tail Carving

Large oblong watermelon needed such as a Charleston Gray. When selecting which side of the watermelon to carve, make sure to use the green and clean side.

Print the stencil on the next page and trim the stencil to a workable size. By cutting slits into the edge of the design, it will be easier to attach to the melon's curved surface.

*See "Watermelon Carving Stencil Usage Instructions" for using stencils, on page 10.*

*Start by using the "Watermelon Carving Step-by-Step Instructions" on pages 13-16.*

## Using Color Code Depth Chart (Colors of a Watermelon )

By using the color code depth chart shown below on the watermelon, you will know how deep to carve, and which colors to make certain cuts.

*Pay attention to colors. Practice using different colors for contrast.*

## Color Code Depth Chart

A = Outside Green Flesh Color
B = Inside Red Flesh Color
C = Inside White Flesh Color
(White color can be made by carving just below the green color outside flesh.)

## Decorating Your Watermelon Carving

Start by using the "Watermelon Carving Decorating Instructions" and ideas on page 17, and by using what you have on hand.

## Special Carving Instructions

Carve Pelican in color code "A".
Carve Fish Tail in color code "C".
Carve all inside lines in color code "B".

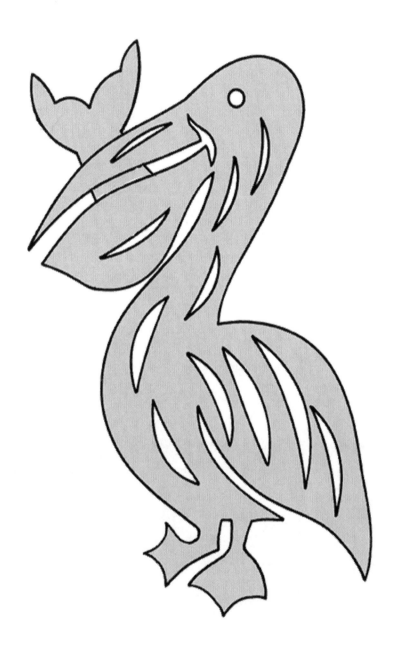

# Pink Flamingo Carving

Large oblong watermelon needed such as a Charleston Gray. When selecting which side of the watermelon to carve, make sure to use the green and clean side.

Print the stencil on the next page and trim the stencil to a workable size. By cutting slits into the edge of the design, it will be easier to attach to the melon's curved surface.

*See "Watermelon Carving Stencil Usage Instructions" for using stencils, on page 10.*

*Start by using the "Watermelon Carving Step-by-Step Instructions" on pages 13-16.*

## Using Color Code Depth Chart (Colors of a Watermelon )

By using the color code depth chart shown below on the watermelon, you will know how deep to carve, and which colors to make certain cuts.

*Pay attention to colors. Practice using different colors for contrast.*

## Color Code Depth Chart

A = Outside Green Flesh Color
B = Inside Red Flesh Color
C = Inside White Flesh Color
(White color can be made by carving just below the green color outside flesh.)

## Decorating Your Watermelon Carving

Start by using the "Watermelon Carving Decorating Instructions" and ideas on page 17, and by using what you have on hand.

## Special Carving Instructions

Carve Pink Flamingo in color code "C".
Carve Grass in color code "A".
Carve all inside lines in color code "B".

# Celebration Rose Carving

Large oblong watermelon needed such as a Charleston Gray. When selecting which side of the watermelon to carve, make sure to use the green and clean side.

Print the stencil on the next page and trim the stencil to a workable size. By cutting slits into the edge of the design, it will be easier to attach to the melon's curved surface.

*See "Watermelon Carving Stencil Usage Instructions" for using stencils, on page 10.*

*Start by using the "Watermelon Carving Step-by-Step Instructions" on pages 13-16.*

## Using Color Code Depth Chart (Colors of a Watermelon )

By using the color code depth chart shown below on the watermelon, you will know how deep to carve, and which colors to make certain cuts.

*Pay attention to colors. Practice using different colors for contrast.*

## Color Code Depth Chart

A = Outside Green Flesh Color
B = Inside Red Flesh Color
C = Inside White Flesh Color
(White color can be made by carving just below the green color outside flesh.)

## Decorating Your Watermelon Carving

Start by using the "Watermelon Carving Decorating Instructions" and ideas on page 17, and by using what you have on hand.

## Special Carving Instructions

Carve Celebration Rose Carvings in color code "A" or "C".
Carve all inside lines in color code "B".

# St. Patrick's Shamrock Carving

Large oblong watermelon needed such as a Charleston Gray. When selecting which side of the watermelon to carve, make sure to use the green and clean side.

Print the stencil on the next page and trim the stencil to a workable size. By cutting slits into the edge of the design, it will be easier to attach to the melon's curved surface.

*See "Watermelon Carving Stencil Usage Instructions" for using stencils, on page 10.*
*Start by using the "Watermelon Carving Step-by-Step Instructions" on pages 13-16.*

## Using Color Code Depth Chart (Colors of a Watermelon )

By using the color code depth chart shown below on the watermelon, you will know how deep to carve, and which colors to make certain cuts.

*Pay attention to colors. Practice using different colors for contrast.*

## Color Code Depth Chart

A = Outside Green Flesh Color
B = Inside Red Flesh Color
C = Inside White Flesh Color
(White color can be made by carving just below the green color outside flesh.)

## Decorating Your Watermelon Carving

Start by using the "Watermelon Carving Decorating Instructions" and ideas on page 17, and by using what you have on hand.

## Special Carving Instructions

Carve St. Patrick's Shamrock in color code "A".
Carve all inside lines in color code "B".

# Scallop Sea Shell Carving

Large oblong watermelon needed such as a Charleston Gray. When selecting which side of the watermelon to carve, make sure to use the green and clean side.

Print the stencil on the next page and trim the stencil to a workable size. By cutting slits into the edge of the design, it will be easier to attach to the melon's curved surface.

*See "Watermelon Carving Stencil Usage Instructions" for using stencils, on page 10.*
*Start by using the "Watermelon Carving Step-by-Step Instructions" on pages 13-16.*

## Using Color Code Depth Chart (Colors of a Watermelon )

By using the color code depth chart shown below on the watermelon, you will know how deep to carve, and which colors to make certain cuts.

*Pay attention to colors. Practice using different colors for contrast.*

## Color Code Depth Chart

A = Outside Green Flesh Color
B = Inside Red Flesh Color
C = Inside White Flesh Color
(White color can be made by carving just below the green color outside flesh.)

## Decorating Your Watermelon Carving

Start by using the "Watermelon Carving Decorating Instructions" and ideas on page 17, and by using what you have on hand.

Special Carving Instructions
Carve Scallop Shell in color code "A" or "C".
Carve all inside lines in color code "B".

# Duo Salmon with Scallop Sea Shell Carving

Large oblong watermelon needed such as a Charleston Gray. When selecting which side of the watermelon to carve, make sure to use the green and clean side.

Print the stencil on the next page and trim the stencil to a workable size. By cutting slits into the edge of the design, it will be easier to attach to the melon's curved surface.

*See "Watermelon Carving Stencil Usage Instructions" for using stencils, on page 10.*
*Start by using the "Watermelon Carving Step-by-Step Instructions" on pages 13-16.*

## Using Color Code Depth Chart (Colors of a Watermelon )

By using the color code depth chart shown below on the watermelon, you will know how deep to carve, and which colors to make certain cuts.

*Pay attention to colors. Practice using different colors for contrast.*

## Color Code Depth Chart

A = Outside Green Flesh Color
B = Inside Red Flesh Color
C = Inside White Flesh Color
(White color can be made by carving just below the green color outside flesh.)

## Decorating Your Watermelon Carving

Start by using the "Watermelon Carving Decorating Instructions" and ideas on page 17, and by using what you have on hand.

## Special Carving Instructions

Carve Scallop Shell in color code "C".
Carve Two Salmon in color code "A".
Carve all inside lines in color code "B".

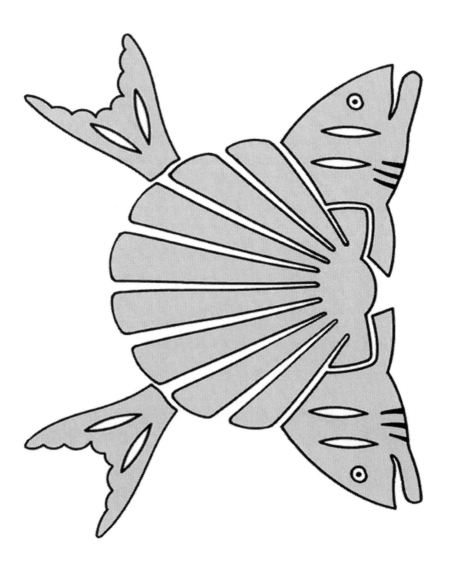

# Eclectic Sea Horse Carving

Large oblong watermelon needed such as a Charleston Gray. When selecting which side of the watermelon to carve, make sure to use the green and clean side.

Print the stencil on the next page and trim the stencil to a workable size. By cutting slits into the edge of the design, it will be easier to attach to the melon's curved surface.

*See "Watermelon Carving Stencil Usage Instructions" for using stencils, on page 10.*
*Start by using the "Watermelon Carving Step-by-Step Instructions" on pages 13-16.*

## Using Color Code Depth Chart (Colors of a Watermelon )

By using the color code depth chart shown below on the watermelon, you will know how deep to carve, and which colors to make certain cuts.

*Pay attention to colors. Practice using different colors for contrast.*

## Color Code Depth Chart

A = Outside Green Flesh Color
B = Inside Red Flesh Color
C = Inside White Flesh Color
(White color can be made by carving just below the green color outside flesh.)

## Decorating Your Watermelon Carving

Start by using the "Watermelon Carving Decorating Instructions" and ideas on page 17, and by using what you have on hand.

## Special Carving Instructions

Carve Eclectic Sea Horse in color code "A" or "C".
Carve all inside lines in color code "B".

# Winter Snowflake Carving

Large oblong watermelon needed such as a Charleston Gray. When selecting which side of the watermelon to carve, make sure to use the green and clean side.

Print the stencil on the next page and trim the stencil to a workable size. By cutting slits into the edge of the design, it will be easier to attach to the melon's curved surface.

*See "Watermelon Carving Stencil Usage Instructions" for using stencils, on page 10.*

*Start by using the "Watermelon Carving Step-by-Step Instructions" on pages 13-16.*

## Using Color Code Depth Chart (Colors of a Watermelon )

By using the color code depth chart shown below on the watermelon, you will know how deep to carve, and which colors to make certain cuts.

***Pay attention to colors. Practice using different colors for contrast.***

## Color Code Depth Chart

> A = Outside Green Flesh Color
> B = Inside Red Flesh Color
> C = Inside White Flesh Color
>> (White color can be made by carving just below the green color outside flesh.)

## Decorating Your Watermelon Carving

Start by using the "Watermelon Carving Decorating Instructions" and ideas on page 17, and by using what you have on hand.

## Special Carving Instructions

> Carve Winter Snowflake in color code "C".
> Carve all inside lines in color code "B".

# Southwestern Coyote Carving

Large oblong watermelon needed such as a Charleston Gray. When selecting which side of the watermelon to carve, make sure to use the green and clean side.

Print the stencil on the next page and trim the stencil to a workable size. By cutting slits into the edge of the design, it will be easier to attach to the melon's curved surface.

*See "Watermelon Carving Stencil Usage Instructions" for using stencils, on page 10.*
*Start by using the "Watermelon Carving Step-by-Step Instructions" on pages 13-16.*

## Using Color Code Depth Chart (Colors of a Watermelon )

By using the color code depth chart shown below on the watermelon, you will know how deep to carve, and which colors to make certain cuts.

*Pay attention to colors. Practice using different colors for contrast.*

## Color Code Depth Chart

A = Outside Green Flesh Color
B = Inside Red Flesh Color
C = Inside White Flesh Color
(White color can be made by carving just below the green color outside flesh.)

## Decorating Your Watermelon Carving

Start by using the "Watermelon Carving Decorating Instructions" and ideas on page 17, and by using what you have on hand.

## Special Carving Instructions

Carve Southwestern Coyote in color code "A" or "C".
Carve all inside lines in color code "B".

# Star of David Carving

Large oblong watermelon needed such as a Charleston Gray. When selecting which side of the watermelon to carve, make sure to use the green and clean side.

Print the stencil on the next page and trim the stencil to a workable size. By cutting slits into the edge of the design, it will be easier to attach to the melon's curved surface.

*See "Watermelon Carving Stencil Usage Instructions" for using stencils, on page 10.*
*Start by using the "Watermelon Carving Step-by-Step Instructions" on pages 13-16.*

## Using Color Code Depth Chart (Colors of a Watermelon )

By using the color code depth chart shown below on the watermelon, you will know how deep to carve, and which colors to make certain cuts.

*Pay attention to colors. Practice using different colors for contrast.*

## Color Code Depth Chart

A = Outside Green Flesh Color
B = Inside Red Flesh Color
C = Inside White Flesh Color
(White color can be made by carving just below the green color outside flesh.)

## Decorating Your Watermelon Carving

Start by using the "Watermelon Carving Decorating Instructions" and ideas on page 17, and by using what you have on hand.

## Special Carving Instructions

Carve Star of David in color code "A".
Carve Bars in color code "C".
Carve all inside lines in color code "B".

# Classic Swan Carving

Large oblong watermelon needed such as a Charleston Gray. When selecting which side of the watermelon to carve, make sure to use the green and clean side.

Print the stencil on the next page and trim the stencil to a workable size. By cutting slits into the edge of the design, it will be easier to attach to the melon's curved surface.

*See "Watermelon Carving Stencil Usage Instructions" for using stencils, on page 10.*
*Start by using the "Watermelon Carving Step-by-Step Instructions" on pages 13-16.*

## Using Color Code Depth Chart (Colors of a Watermelon )

By using the color code depth chart shown below on the watermelon, you will know how deep to carve, and which colors to make certain cuts.

*Pay attention to colors. Practice using different colors for contrast.*

## Color Code Depth Chart

> A = Outside Green Flesh Color
> B = Inside Red Flesh Color
> C = Inside White Flesh Color
> > (White color can be made by carving just below the green color outside flesh.)

## Decorating Your Watermelon Carving

Start by using the "Watermelon Carving Decorating Instructions" and ideas on page 17, and by using what you have on hand.

## Special Carving Instructions

> Carve Classic Swan in color code "A" or "C".
> Carve all inside lines in color code "B".

# I Love You and Kissing Doves Carving

Large oblong watermelon needed such as a Charleston Gray. When selecting which side of the watermelon to carve, make sure to use the green and clean side.

Print the stencil on the next page and trim the stencil to a workable size. By cutting slits into the edge of the design, it will be easier to attach to the melon's curved surface.

*See "Watermelon Carving Stencil Usage Instructions" for using stencils, on page 10.*
*Start by using the "Watermelon Carving Step-by-Step Instructions" on pages 13-16.*

## Using Color Code Depth Chart (Colors of a Watermelon )

By using the color code depth chart shown below on the watermelon, you will know how deep to carve, and which colors to make certain cuts.

*Pay attention to colors. Practice using different colors for contrast.*

## Color Code Depth Chart

> A = Outside Green Flesh Color
> B = Inside Red Flesh Color
> C = Inside White Flesh Color
> (White color can be made by carving just below the green color outside flesh.)

## Decorating Your Watermelon Carving

Start by using the "Watermelon Carving Decorating Instructions" and ideas on page 17, and by using what you have on hand.

## Special Carving Instructions

> Carve I Love You and Kissing Doves in color code "A" or "C".
> Carve all inside lines in color code "B".

# Kissing Swans and Bell Carving

Large oblong watermelon needed such as a Charleston Gray. When selecting which side of the watermelon to carve, make sure to use the green and clean side.

Print the stencil on the next page and trim the stencil to a workable size. By cutting slits into the edge of the design, it will be easier to attach to the melon's curved surface.

*See "Watermelon Carving Stencil Usage Instructions" for using stencils, on page 10.*
*Start by using the "Watermelon Carving Step-by-Step Instructions" on pages 13-16.*

## Using Color Code Depth Chart (Colors of a Watermelon )

By using the color code depth chart shown below on the watermelon, you will know how deep to carve, and which colors to make certain cuts.

*Pay attention to colors. Practice using different colors for contrast.*

## Color Code Depth Chart

A = Outside Green Flesh Color
B = Inside Red Flesh Color
C = Inside White Flesh Color
(White color can be made by carving just below the green color outside flesh.)

## Decorating Your Watermelon Carving

Start by using the "Watermelon Carving Decorating Instructions" and ideas on page 17, and by using what you have on hand.

## Special Carving Instructions

Carve Swans and Bell in color code "A" or "C".
Carve all inside lines in color code "B".

# Nautical Swordfish Carving

Large oblong watermelon needed such as a Charleston Gray. When selecting which side of the watermelon to carve, make sure to use the green and clean side.

Print the stencil on the next page and trim the stencil to a workable size. By cutting slits into the edge of the design, it will be easier to attach to the melon's curved surface.

*See "Watermelon Carving Stencil Usage Instructions" for using stencils, on page 10.*
*Start by using the "Watermelon Carving Step-by-Step Instructions" on pages 13-16.*

## Using Color Code Depth Chart (Colors of a Watermelon )

By using the color code depth chart shown below on the watermelon, you will know how deep to carve, and which colors to make certain cuts.

*Pay attention to colors. Practice using different colors for contrast.*

## Color Code Depth Chart

> A = Outside Green Flesh Color
> B = Inside Red Flesh Color
> C = Inside White Flesh Color
> > (White color can be made by carving just below the green color outside flesh.)

## Decorating Your Watermelon Carving

Start by using the "Watermelon Carving Decorating Instructions" and ideas on page 17, and by using what you have on hand.

## Special Carving Instructions

> Carve Swordfish Carving in color code "A" or "C".
> Carve all inside lines in color code "B".

# Holiday Thanksgiving Ship Carving

Large oblong watermelon needed such as a Charleston Gray. When selecting which side of the watermelon to carve, make sure to use the green and clean side.

Print the stencil on the next page and trim the stencil to a workable size. By cutting slits into the edge of the design, it will be easier to attach to the melon's curved surface.

*See "Watermelon Carving Stencil Usage Instructions" for using stencils, on page 10.*
*Start by using the "Watermelon Carving Step-by-Step Instructions" on pages 13-16.*

## Using Color Code Depth Chart (Colors of a Watermelon )

By using the color code depth chart shown below on the watermelon, you will know how deep to carve, and which colors to make certain cuts.

*Pay attention to colors. Practice using different colors for contrast.*

## Color Code Depth Chart

A = Outside Green Flesh Color
B = Inside Red Flesh Color
C = Inside White Flesh Color
(White color can be made by carving just below the green color outside flesh.)

## Decorating Your Watermelon Carving

Start by using the "Watermelon Carving Decorating Instructions" and ideas on page 17, and by using what you have on hand.

## Special Carving Instructions

Carve Thanksgiving Ship in color code "A".
Carve all inside lines in color code "B".

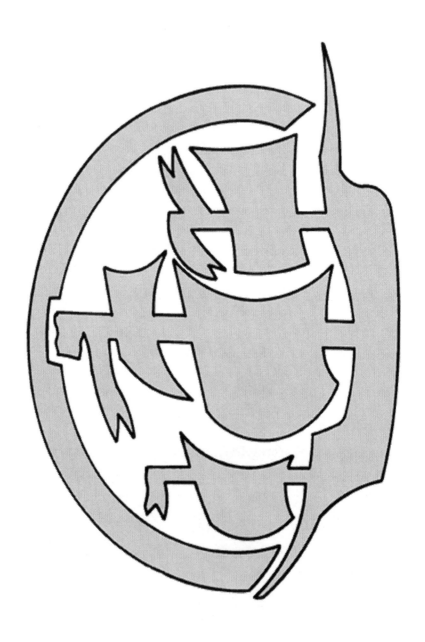

# Three Dolphins and Anchor Carving

Large oblong watermelon needed such as a Charleston Gray. When selecting which side of the watermelon to carve, make sure to use the green and clean side.

Print the stencil on the next page and trim the stencil to a workable size. By cutting slits into the edge of the design, it will be easier to attach to the melon's curved surface.

*See "Watermelon Carving Stencil Usage Instructions" for using stencils, on page 10.*
*Start by using the "Watermelon Carving Step-by-Step Instructions" on pages 13-16.*

## Using Color Code Depth Chart (Colors of a Watermelon )

By using the color code depth chart shown below on the watermelon, you will know how deep to carve, and which colors to make certain cuts.

*Pay attention to colors. Practice using different colors for contrast.*

## Color Code Depth Chart

A = Outside Green Flesh Color
B = Inside Red Flesh Color
C = Inside White Flesh Color
(White color can be made by carving just below the green color outside flesh.)

## Decorating Your Watermelon Carving

Start by using the "Watermelon Carving Decorating Instructions" and ideas on page 17, and by using what you have on hand.

## Special Carving Instructions

Carve Three Dolphins and Anchor in color code "A" or "C".
Carve all inside lines in color code "B".

# U.S.A. Carving

Large oblong watermelon needed such as a Charleston Gray. When selecting which side of the watermelon to carve, make sure to use the green and clean side.
Print the stencil on the next page and trim the stencil to a workable size. By cutting slits into the edge of the design, it will be easier to attach to the melon's curved surface.

*See "Watermelon Carving Stencil Usage Instructions" for using stencils, on page 10.*
*Start by using the "Watermelon Carving Step-by-Step Instructions" on pages 13-16.*

## Using Color Code Depth Chart (Colors of a Watermelon )

By using the color code depth chart shown below on the watermelon, you will know how deep to carve, and which colors to make certain cuts.

*Pay attention to colors. Practice using different colors for contrast.*

## Color Code Depth Chart

> A = Outside Green Flesh Color
> B = Inside Red Flesh Color
> C = Inside White Flesh Color
> > (White color can be made by carving just below the green color outside flesh.)

## Decorating Your Watermelon Carving

Start by using the "Watermelon Carving Decorating Instructions" and ideas on page 17, and by using what you have on hand.

## Special Carving Instructions

> Carve U.S.A. Carving in color code "C".
> Carve all inside lines in color code "B".

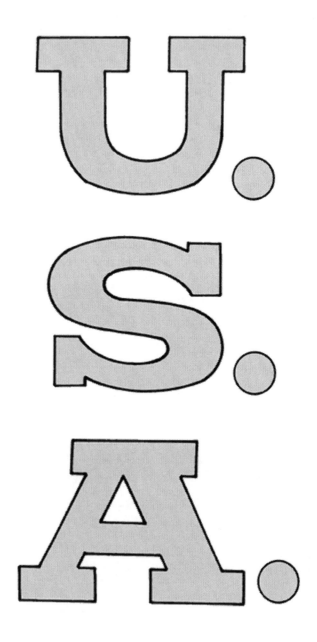

# Classical Vase Carving

Large oblong watermelon needed such as a Charleston Gray. When selecting which side of the watermelon to carve, make sure to use the green and clean side.

Print the stencil on the next page and trim the stencil to a workable size. By cutting slits into the edge of the design, it will be easier to attach to the melon's curved surface.

*See "Watermelon Carving Stencil Usage Instructions" for using stencils, on page 10.*
*Start by using the "Watermelon Carving Step-by-Step Instructions" on pages 13-16.*

## Using Color Code Depth Chart (Colors of a Watermelon )

By using the color code depth chart shown below on the watermelon, you will know how deep to carve, and which colors to make certain cuts.

*Pay attention to colors. Practice using different colors for contrast.*

## Color Code Depth Chart

> A = Outside Green Flesh Color
> B = Inside Red Flesh Color
> C = Inside White Flesh Color
>> (White color can be made by carving just below the green color outside flesh.)

## Decorating Your Watermelon Carving

Start by using the "Watermelon Carving Decorating Instructions" and ideas on page 17, and by using what you have on hand.

## Special Carving Instructions

> Carve Classical Vase in color code "A" or "C".
> Carve all inside lines in color code "B".

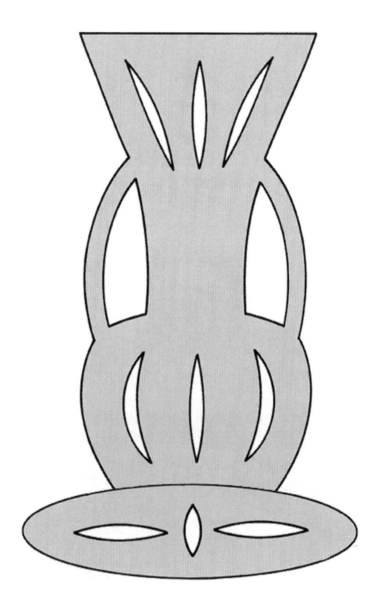

# Eclectic Vase Carving

Large oblong watermelon needed such as a Charleston Gray. When selecting which side of the watermelon to carve, make sure to use the green and clean side.

Print the stencil on the next page and trim the stencil to a workable size. By cutting slits into the edge of the design, it will be easier to attach to the melon's curved surface.

*See "Watermelon Carving Stencil Usage Instructions" for using stencils, on page 10.*
*Start by using the "Watermelon Carving Step-by-Step Instructions" on pages 13-16.*

## Using Color Code Depth Chart (Colors of a Watermelon )

By using the color code depth chart shown below on the watermelon, you will know how deep to carve, and which colors to make certain cuts.

*Pay attention to colors. Practice using different colors for contrast.*

## Color Code Depth Chart

A = Outside Green Flesh Color
B = Inside Red Flesh Color
C = Inside White Flesh Color
     (White color can be made by carving just below the green
     color outside flesh.)

## Decorating Your Watermelon Carving

Start by using the "Watermelon Carving Decorating Instructions" and ideas on page 17, and by using what you have on hand.

## Special Carving Instructions

Carve Eclectic Vase in color code "A" OR "C".
Carve all inside lines in color code "B".

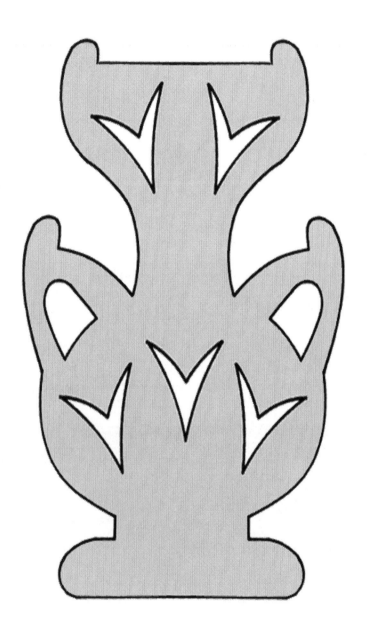

# Wedding Bell Carving

Large oblong watermelon needed such as a Charleston Gray. When selecting which side of the watermelon to carve, make sure to use the green and clean side.

Print the stencil on the next page and trim the stencil to a workable size. By cutting slits into the edge of the design, it will be easier to attach to the melon's curved surface.

*See "Watermelon Carving Stencil Usage Instructions" for using stencils, on page 10.*
*Start by using the "Watermelon Carving Step-by-Step Instructions" on pages 13-16.*

## Using Color Code Depth Chart (Colors of a Watermelon )

By using the color code depth chart shown below on the watermelon, you will know how deep to carve, and which colors to make certain cuts.

*Pay attention to colors. Practice using different colors for contrast.*

## Color Code Depth Chart

> A = Outside Green Flesh Color
> B = Inside Red Flesh Color
> C = Inside White Flesh Color
>> (White color can be made by carving just below the green color outside flesh.)

## Decorating Your Watermelon Carving

Start by using the "Watermelon Carving Decorating Instructions" and ideas on page 18, and by using what you have on hand.

## Special Carving Instructions

> Carve Wedding Bells in color code "C".
> Carve all inside lines in color code "B".

# Lonnie Lynch: Celebrity Chef and Author

A master, talented, skilled, imaginative- these are just a few of the words used to describe Lonnie Lynch and his prowess for creating fabulous food. The author of three cookbooks, Mastering the Art of Florida Seafood, "Easy" Melon Carvings, and "Easy" Watermelon Carvings, Lonnie now introduces his fourth and latest book, Seductive and Sinful Cooking. With over 20 years of experience as a cook, Lonnie Lynch has worked in fine hotels, restaurants and country clubs. He is a well known regional chef who has mastered the art of cooking seafood, carving melons and now unlocks the secret to the art of seduction and romantic dinners. In his latest tome, he dishes up the inside secrets of food seduction as a culinary cuisine in a creative, fun and unique way.

*Lonnie's experience far surpasses that of other local chefs. Lonnie has worked with Henry Boubee of Windows of the World and the Ritz Carlton, Walter Schieb, executive chef of the White House and the talented Steve Galluzi of Pete's and Caesar's Palace.*

Raised just outside Chicago, Lonnie has also lived in California and Texas and picked up the local cuisine's southwest flair along the way. He has refined his culinary skills at fine establishments such as Houston's, Stetson's, the Registry Hotel in Dallas, Five Star & Five Diamond, the Boca Raton Hotel and Resort and the showcase kitchen at Pete's Restaurant in Boca Raton, Florida. Residing in Florida since 1986, Lonnie has honed his skills as a fabulous seafood chef and as an expert with fresh, local cuisine. 1989 was a turning point for the master chef when he listened to the Tony Robbins Power tapes, Take Charge of Your Life. They greatly inspired and influenced him to get his passion for cooking out to the world in book form and share his vast knowledge of great cuisine.

Now, having been a chef at over 300 weddings, the couples who were in love inspired him to write his latest book, Seductive and Sinful Cooking so he could bring together the two finest things life has to offer- romance and food. He has combined the customs of seduction and the time-honored practices of cooking to make a sensual, inviting experience couples can share. One of the most thorough books on culinary seduction and romantic dinners you could ever hope to read, Seductive and Sinful Cooking shows you what works and helps you create your own style of romantic language through the use of food and presentation..

# Sun-Sentinel 4th July Article

## *Carving by the book: It's easy*

## *By Deborah S. Hartz, Food Editor*

He has carved a smiling Mickey Mouse, a skull and crossbones, an ancient Chinaman and even a baby grand piano. But his medium isn't wood or marble. It's watermelon.

Lonnie Lynch, sous chef at the Aberdeen Country Club in Boynton Beach, has spent the past five years perfecting his art on more than 400 watermelons. And now he tells how to carve melons at home in his book Carving Watermelon Centerpieces.

You can use carved watermelons to decorate a buffet table or serve instead of cake at a child's birthday party. It's simple to do and impressive to look at.

You can carve the melon the day before your party if you wrap it in plastic and keep it in the refrigerator. And, if you want to actually serve the carving, "just whack off the front of the melon, save your carving and cut up the back half to eat," Lynch says.

Lynch began his craft in 1986 while working with a friend who was garde manger at the Boca Raton Hotel and Club. "I'd pick up a knife and carve a couple of melons, then I'd grab a chain saw and carve ice. The ice was a disaster," he says. But the melons were a big success.

In 1988, when he went work at Pete's, Boca Raton a restaurant in Boca Raton, his melons were displayed each weekend. "The best part was the people would come in and say, "I like this one," or "That's the best one you've done," or 'I couldn't do that," says Lynch, who has since perfected his ice-carving skills.

Because people were so interested, he invested $8,000 of his own to produce a book of Instructions on carving. Looking through it recently, I decided to try my luck.

"You're going to have problems on the first one, but with practice and patience it gets easier," he warned me. As it turned out, the warning was unnecessary.

My first step was to gather the needed equipment: a sharp paring knife (from my kitchen drawer), a V-shaped vegetable cutting tool (which I happened to have on hand but which can be purchased at restaurant supply stores) and a heavy-duty X-Acto knife (available at office supply stores).

# Cutting up with melon carving surprisingly easy

Then I found the perfect watermelon: large, long and regular in color and shape. Although there are 150 varieties of watermelons, Lynch suggests that beginners use the Charleston Gray because of its large size: 16 to 35 pounds. (I used a Royal sweet, a variety of Jubilee, because it was on sale at the supermarket the week I shopped; it worked fine.)

Next, I traced a pattern from the book onto a piece of paper. The patterns look like something you would find in a child's coloring book: simple, graphic and heavily outlined.

I picked a horse's head because it didn't have many intricate areas where a knife could slip and remove a key body part. But if your knife does slip while you are working, don't worry: There's a section in the book on repairs. For instance, flowers can hide problem areas, and toothpicks can help reattach lopped-off ears, Lynch says.

Lynch recommends that, in addition to the horse, beginners try his rose, Chinese character, vase or swan patterns because of their simplicity.

Soon, with practice and confidence, you will be carving the more intricate designs, such as dolphins jumping from waves, flying dragons, Stars of David, Easter bunnies and Christmas trees, Lynch says. (Melons imported from Mexico are available year round - including at Christmastime.)

Once you trace the pattern, secure the stencil to the melon with Scotch tape ( this was the only brand I could find that actually stuck to the sweating melon). Then trace the patterns lines with the X-Acto knife, scoring the rind of the watermelon.

At this point, I encountered my one problem carving the melon: Because I was working outside on my balcony (to avoid any mess in the kitchen,) the humid air caused the chilled melon to sweat and the dampness began to dissolve the paper pattern, Lynch suggests working in an air-conditioned space (and there really was no mess, so I could have done the carving indoors).

Once the pattern was scored into the melon, I found that deepening the traced cuts with the paring knife and finishing the edges with the V-shaped tool were a snap. The entire process - from tracing the pattern to finishing the carving --took me about an hour. Not bad for a beginner, Lynch says. Although, he adds he could have done it in 10-15 minutes.

# — Mastering The Art Of —
# Florida Seafood

## Published by Pineapple Press

## From Palm Beach County, Florida Comes a Unique Collection of Seafood Recipes!

Lonnie is now ready to teach you the secrets he learned while preparing seafood in such fine eating establishments as the Boca Raton Hotel & Resort, Pete's Boca Raton, Famous Firehouse Rest., Santa Fe Grille, Nick's Italian Fishery and Palm Beach County country clubs, such as Aberdeen and Bocaire. From Stoned Crabs to Pompano, from Orange Pecan Barbecue Sauce to Old Floridian Grill Seasonings, Lonnie will teach you

Mastering The Art Of Florida Seafood is a superb collection of seafood recipes that also offers the kitchen cook tips on purchasing seafood, preparing and serving fish and shellfish (and even alligators!). This anthology of fun, nutritious, and delicious dining is replete with suggestions for the culinary art of food placement and presentation. From Orange-Pecan Barbecue Sauce, Caesar Salad with Blackened Pepper Shrimp, and Lobster Lisa with a Sherry-and-Brandy Mornay Sauce, to Stuffed Dolphin Florentine with Creamy Artichoke Sauce, Shrimp and Broccoli with Roasted Garlic and Red Peppers, and Oysters Palm Beach with Balsamic Hot Bacon Sauce, Mastering The Art Of Florida Seafood is a compendium of marvelous meal seafood ideas that would grace any table and satisfy any palate. Help other customers find the most helpful reviews.

Chef Lonnie Lynch, shares his secrets on how to master the art of preparing and presenting Florida's sea's full of delicious seafood. Included are tips on purchasing, preparing, and serving fish and shellfish. Cooking is fun! Chef Lynch illustrates artistic food placement, food painting techniques, and more. This cookbook is chock-full of scrumptious recipes, from appetizers to desserts that complement these tantalizing seafood dishes.

*Paperback $14.95 Size: 6 x 9 144 Pages B&W illustrations*
*ISBN: 1-56164-176-6 ISBN-13: 978-1561641765*
*Contact the order department at 800-746-3275, ext 10*
*http://www.pineapplepress.com/ or http://www.amazon.com/*

# Seductive and Sinful Cooking

From the Columns of Paideia comes the most anticipated tome in years. By means of the "VII Columns of Seduction," you're literally bestowed the keys to the seduction and romantic dinner kingdom way of life. You will gain knowledge of secret, seductive recipes and mysterious, uplifting effects to make you more desirable and playful. Discover how we keep our relationships lively and enchanting!

What are the VII Columns of Seduction and how do they transmit to seduction and creating a romantic dinner? In this tome, the "Seductive and Sinful Cooking", you will acquire the wisdom of the VII Columns of Seduction as they allow us to observe the manner in which they correlate to us on a day-by-day basis in our interactions.

**The VII Columns of Seduction**
*Column I Seduction Theory*
*Column II Legendary Wisdom*
*Column III Enchanting Traditions*
*Column IV Passion Philosophy*
*Column V Culinary Flamboyance*
*Column VI Exquisite Potions*
*Column VII Epicurean Recipes*

Your lover will think you are an epicurean god or goddess who has arrived to mysteriously give them a tantalizing culinary feast. Everybody desires someone who can step outside of his or her box and is mysterious enough to move their inner passion. They want someone who can take them in, slowly tease, intrigue them, entice their emotions, and make them experience novel thoughts and utter feelings that they would have never experienced before or thought they would ever experience.

With this new knowledge, you will enhance your mastery of epicurean enticement, gain a greater understanding of human psychology, and learn poetic dynamics—this will, in turn, increase social interaction. Bear in mind, seduction is really about interconnecting in a new potent way that makes you (and your beliefs) irresistible to others. They won't be able to help but want to pay attention to more of what you have to offer! These secrets are no longer secrets to you, as you now carry them with you always, like the ancient crystal phials.

25723047R00066

Made in the USA
Middletown, DE
08 November 2015